AS A
MAN THINKETH

SOME CURRENT AND FORTHCOMING SUN BOOKS

REPRINTS OF ORISON SWETT MARDEN BOOKS

AN IRON WILL
CHARACTER: The Grandest Thing in the World
THE EXCEPTIONAL EMPLOYEE
EVERY MAN A KING or MIGHT IN MIND-
   MASTERY
HE CAN WHO THINKS HE CAN
THE HOUR OF OPPORTUNITY
HOW THEY SUCCEEDED
HOW TO GET WHAT YOU WANT

THE MIRACLE OF RIGHT THOUGHT
THE OPTIMISTIC LIFE
PEACE, POWER, AND PLENTY
PUSHING TO THE FRONT VOL I
PUSHING TO THE FRONT VOL II
THE SECRET OF ACHIEVEMENT
SELLING THINGS
YOU CAN, BUT WILL YOU?
WHY GROW OLD?

JAMES ALLEN BOOKS

ABOVE LIFE'S TURMOIL
ALL THESE THINGS ADDED
AS A MAN THINKETH
EIGHT PILLARS OF PROSPERITY
FROM POVERTY TO POWER
THE LIFE TRIUMPHANT
LIGHT ON LIFE'S DIFFICULTIES
MAN: KING OF MIND, BODY AND
   CIRCUMSTANCE

THE MASTERY OF DESTINY
MEDITATIONS: A YEAR BOOK
MORNING AND EVENING THOUGHTS
OUT FROM THE HEART
THROUGH THE GATE OF GOOD
THE WAY OF PEACE
PERSONALITY: ITS CULTIVATION AND
   POWER AND HOW TO ATTAIN
   (by Lily L. Allen)

RALPH WALDO TRINE BOOKS

CHARACTER BUILDING THOUGHT POWER
EVERY LIVING CREATURE or Heart Training
   Through the Animal World
IN THE FIRE OF THE HEART
THE GREATEST THING EVER KNOWN

THE HIGHER POWERS OF MIND & SPIRIT
THE MAN WHO KNEW
ON THE OPEN ROAD - Being Some Thoughts
   and a Little Creed of Wholesome Living
THIS MYSTICAL LIFE OF OURS

ADDITIONAL IMPORTANT TITLES

BEING AND BECOMING: Principles and Practices of the Science of Spirit by F.L. Holmes.
CREATIVE MIND by Ernest S. Holmes.
HEALTH AND WEALTH FROM WITHIN by William E. Towne.
A MESSAGE TO GARCIA and Other Essays by Elbert Hubbard.
POSITIVE THOUGHTS ATTRACT SUCCESS by Mary A. Dodson and Ella E. Dodson.
THE SCIENCE OF GETTING RICH: or Financial Success Through Creative Thought.
SELF MASTERY THROUGH CONSCIOUS AUTOSUGGESTION by Emile Coué.
HOW TO PRACTICE SUGGESTION AND AUTOSUGGESTION by Emile Coué.
MY METHOD by Emile Coué.
THE SUCCESS PROCESS by Brown Landone.
THE GIFT OF THE SPIRIT by Prentice Mulford.
THE GIFT OF UNDERSTANDING by Prentice Mulford.
THOUGHT FORCES by Prentice Mulford.   THOUGHTS ARE THINGS by Prentice Mulford.
VISUALIZATION AND CONCENTRATION and How to Choose a Career by F.L. Holmes.

For a list of all currently available Sun Books Titles, write to:
Booklist, PO Box 5588, Santa Fe NM 87502-5588

As a
Man Thinketh

By
James Allen

SUN BOOKS
Sun Publishing Company
Santa Fe, N.M.

First Sun Books Printing—April 1983
Second Sun Books Printing--1984 Mar
Third Sun Books Printing – 2008 Aug

Sun Books
Sun Publishing Company
P.O. Box 5588
Santa Fe, New Mexico 87502-5588 U.S.A

ISBN: 0-89540-136-3
SB-136

MANUFACTURED IN THE
UNITED STATES OF AMERICA

CONTENTS

AS A
MAN THINKETH

FOREWORD

THIS little volume (the result of meditation and experience) is not intended as an exhaustive treatise on the much-written-upon subject of the power of thought. It is suggestive rather than explanatory, its object being to stimulate men and women to the discovery and perception of the truth that—

"They themselves are makers of themselves"

by virtue of the thoughts which they choose and encourage; that mind is the master-weaver, both of the inner garment of character and the outer garment of circumstance, and that, as they may have hitherto woven in ignorance and pain they may now weave in enlightenment and happiness.

JAMES ALLEN

As a
Man Thinketh

THOUGHT AND CHARACTER

THE aphorism, "As a man thinketh in his heart so is he," not only embraces the whole of a man's being, but is so comprehensive as to reach out to every condition and circumstance of his life. A man is literally *what he thinks*, his character being the complete sum of all his thoughts.

As the plant springs from, and could not be without, the seed, so every act of a man springs from the hidden seeds of thought, and could not have appeared without them. This applies equally to those acts called "spontaneous" and "unpremeditated" as to those which are deliberately executed.

Act is the blossom of thought, and joy and suffering are its fruits; thus does a man garner in the sweet and bitter fruitage of his own husbandry.

"Thought in the mind hath made us. What we are
By thought was wrought and built. If a man's mind
Hath evil thoughts, pain comes on him as comes
The wheel the ox behind. . . .
      If one endure
In purity of thought, joy follows him
As his own shadow—sure."

Man is a growth by law, and not a creation by artifice, and cause and effect is as absolute and undeviating in the hidden realm of thought as in the world of visible and material things. A noble and Godlike character is not a thing of favour or chance, but is the natural result of continued effort in right thinking, the effect of long-cherished association with Godlike thoughts. An ignoble and bestial character, by the same process, is the result of the continued harbouring of grovelling thoughts.

Man is made or unmade by himself; in the armoury of thought he forges the weapons by which he destroys himself; he also fashions the tools with which he builds for himself heavenly mansions of joy and strength and peace. By the right choice and true application of thought, man ascends to the Divine Perfection; by the abuse and wrong application of thought, he descends below the level of the beast. Between these two extremes are all the grades of character, and man is their maker and master.

Of all the beautiful truths pertaining to the soul which have been restored and brought to light in this age, none is more gladdening or fruitful of divine promise and confidence than this—that man is the master of thought, the moulder of character, and the maker and shaper of condition, environment, and destiny.

As a being of Power, Intelligence, and Love, and the lord of his own thoughts, man holds the key to every situation, and contains within himself that transforming and regenerative agency by which he may make himself what he wills.

Man is always the master, even in his weakest and most abandoned state; but in his weakness and degradation he is the foolish master who misgoverns his "household." When he begins to reflect upon his condition, and to search diligently for the Law upon which his being is established, he then becomes the wise master, directing his energies with intelligence, and fashioning his thoughts to fruitful issues. Such is the *conscious* master, and man can only thus become by discovering *within himself* the laws of thought; which discovery is totally a matter of application, self-analysis, and experience.

Only by much searching and mining are gold and diamonds obtained, and man can find every truth connected with his being if he will dig deep into the mine of his soul; and that he is the maker of his character, the moulder of his life, and the builder of his destiny, he may unerringly prove, if he will watch, control, and alter his thoughts, tracing their effects upon himself, upon others, and upon his life and circumstances, linking cause and effect by patient practice and investigation, and utilizing his every experience, even to the most trivial, every-day occurrence, as a means of obtaining that knowledge of himself which is Understanding,

Wisdom, Power. In this direction, as in no other, is the law absolute that "He that seeketh findeth; and to him that knocketh it shall be opened"; for only by patience, practice, and ceaseless importunity can a man enter the Door of the Temple of Knowledge.

EFFECT OF THOUGHT
ON CIRCUMSTANCES

A MAN'S mind may be likened to a garden, which may be intelligently cultivated or allowed to run wild; but whether cultivated or neglected, it must, and will, *bring forth*. If no useful seeds are *put* into it, then an abundance of useless weed-seeds will *fall* therein, and will continue to produce their kind.

Just as a gardener cultivates his plot, keeping it free from weeds, and growing the flowers and fruits which

14

he requires, so may a man tend the garden of his mind, weeding out all the wrong, useless, and impure thoughts, and cultivating toward perfection the flowers and fruits of right, useful, and pure thoughts. By pursuing thi process, a man sooner or later discovers that he is the master-gardener of his soul, the director of his life. He also reveals, within himself, the laws of thought, and understands, with ever-increasing accuracy, how the thought-forces and mind-elements operate in the shaping of his character, circumstances, and destiny.

Thought and character are one, and as character can only manifest and discover itself through environment and circumstance, the outer conditions of

15

a person's life will always be found
to be harmoniously related to his inner state. This does not mean that a
man's circumstances at any given time
are an indication of his *entire* character, but that those circumstances are
so intimately connected with some
vital thought-element within himself
that, for the time being, they are in-
dispensable to his development.

Every man is where he is by the
law of his being; the thoughts which
he has built into his character have
brought him there, and in the arrange-
ment of his life there is no element
of chance, but all is the result of a
law which cannot err. This is just
as true of those who feel "out of harmony" with their surroundings as of

16

those who are contented with them.

As a progressive and evolving being, man is where he is that he may learn that he may grow; and as he learns the spiritual lesson which any circumstance contains for him, it passes away and gives place to other circumstances.

Man is buffeted by circumstances so long as he believes himself to be the creature of outside conditions, but when he realizes he is a creative power, and that he may command the hidden soil and seeds of his being out of which circumstances grow, he then becomes the rightful master of himself.

That circumstances *grow* out of thought every man knows who has for any length of time practised self-control and self-purification, for he will have noticed that the alteration in his circumstances has been in exact ratio with his altered mental condition. So true is this that when a man earnestly applies himself to remedy the defects in his character, and makes swift and marked progress, he passes rapidly through a succession of vicissitudes.

The soul attracts that which it secretly harbours; that which it loves, and also that which it fears; it reaches the height of its cherished aspirations; it falls to the level of its unchastened desires,—and circumstances are the means by which the soul receives its own.

Every thought-seed sown or allowed to fall into the mind, and to take root there, produces its own, blossoming

18

sooner or later into act, and bearing its own fruitage of opportunity and circumstance. Good thoughts bear good fruit, bad thoughts bad fruit.

The outer world of circumstance shapes itself to the inner world of thought, and both pleasant and unpleasant external conditions are factors which make for the ultimate good of the individual. As the reaper of his own harvest, man learns both by suffering and bliss.

Following the inmost desires, aspirations, thoughts, by which he allows himself to be dominated (pursuing the will-o'-the-wisps of impure imaginings or steadfastly walking the highway of strong and high endeavor), a man at last arrives at their fruition and fulfilment in the outer conditions of his life. The laws of growth and adjustment everywhere obtain.

A man does not come to the alms-house or the jail by the tyranny of fate or circumstance, but by the pathway of grovelling thoughts and base desires. Neither does a pure-minded man fall suddenly into crime by stress of any mere external force; the criminal thought had long been secretly fostered in the heart, and the hour of opportunity revealed its gathered power. Circumstance does not make the man; it reveals him to himself. No such conditions can exist as descending into vice and its attendant sufferings apart from vicious inclinations, or ascending into virtue and its pure happiness without the continued cultivation of virtuous aspirations; and man, therefore, as the lord and master of thought, is the maker of himself, the shaper and author of environment. Even at birth the soul comes to its own, and through every step of its earthly pilgrimage it attracts those combinations of conditions which reveal itself, which are the reflections of its own purity and impurity, its strength and weakness.

Men do not attract that which they *want*, but that which they *are*. Their whims, fancies, and ambitions are thwarted at every step, but their inmost thoughts and desires are fed with their own food, be it foul or clean. The "divinity that shapes our ends" is in ourselves; it is our very

self. Man is manacled only by himself: thought and action are the jailers
of Fate—they imprison, being base
they are also the angels of Freedom—
they liberate, being noble. Not what
he wishes and prays for does a man get,
but what he justly earns. His wishes
and prayers are only gratified and answered when they harmonize with his
thoughts and actions.

In the light of this truth, what,
then, is the meaning of "fighting
against circumstances"? It means
that a man is continually revolting
against an *effect* without, while all the
time he is nourishing and preserving
its *cause* in his heart. That cause may
take the form of a conscious vice or an
unconscious weakness; but whatever it

is, it stubbornly retards the efforts of its possessor, and thus calls aloud for remedy.

Men are anxious to improve their circumstances, but are unwilling to improve themselves; they therefore remain bound. The man who does not shrink from self-crucifixion can never fail to accomplish the object upon which his heart is set. This is as true of earthly as of heavenly things. Even the man whose sole object is to acquire wealth must be prepared to make great personal sacrifices before he can accomplish his object; and how much more so he who would realize a strong and well-poised life?

Here is a man who is wretchedly poor. He is extremely anxious that his surroundings and home comforts should be improved, yet all the time he shirks his work, and considers he is justified in trying to deceive his employer on the ground of the insufficiency of his wages. Such a man does not understand the simplest rudiments of those principles which are the basis of true prosperity, and is not only totally unfitted to rise out of his wretchedness, but is actually attracting to himself a still deeper wretchedness by dwelling in, and acting out, indolent, deceptive, and unmanly thoughts.

Here is a rich man who is the victim of a painful and persistent disease as the result of gluttony. He is willing to give large sums of money to get rid of it, but he will not sacrifice his gluttonous desires. He wants to gratify his taste for rich and unnatural viands and have his health as well. Such a man is totally unfit to have health, because he has not yet learned the first principles of a healthy life.

Here is an employer of labour who adopts crooked measures to avoid paying the regulation wage, and, in the hope of making larger profits, reduces the wages of his work-people. Such a man is altogether unfitted for prosperity, and when he finds himself bankrupt, both as regards reputation and riches, he blames circumstances, not knowing that he is the sole author of his condition.

I have introduced these three cases merely as illustrative of the truth that man is the causer (though nearly always unconsciously) of his circumstances, and that, whilst aiming at a good end, he is continually frustrating its accomplishment by encouraging thoughts and desires which cannot possibly harmonize with that end. Such cases could be multiplied and varied almost indefinitely, but this is not necessary, as the reader can, if he so resolves, trace the action of the laws of thought in his own mind and life, and until this is done, mere external facts cannot serve as a ground of reasoning.

Circumstances, however, are so complicated, thought is so deeply rooted, and the conditions of happiness vary so vastly with individuals, that a

26

man's *entire* soul-condition (although it may be known to himself) cannot be judged by another from the external aspect of his life alone. A man may be honest in certain directions, yet suffer privations; a man may be dishonest in certain directions, yet acquire wealth; but the conclusion usually formed that the one man fails *because of his particular honesty*, and that the other prospers *because of his particular dishonesty*, is the result of a superficial judgment, which assumes that the dishonest man is almost totally corrupt, and the honest man almost entirely virtuous. In the light of a deeper knowledge and wider experience, such judgment is found to be erroneous. The dishonest man may have some admirable virtues which the other does not possess; and the honest man obnoxious vices which are absent in the other. The honest man reaps the good results of his honest thoughts and acts; he also brings upon himself the sufferings which his vices produce. The dishonest man likewise garners his own suffering and happiness.

It is pleasing to human vanity to believe that one suffers because of one's virtue; but not until a man has extirpated every sickly, bitter, and impure thought from his mind, and washed every sinful stain from his soul, can he be in a position to know and declare that his sufferings are the result of his good, and not of his bad

28

qualities; and on the way to, yet long before he has reached, that supreme perfection, he will have found, working in his mind and life, the Great Law which is absolutely just, and which cannot, therefore, give good for evil, evil for good. Possessed of such knowledge, he will then know, looking back upon his past ignorance and blindness, that his life is, and always was, justly ordered, and that all his past experiences, good and bad, were the equitable outworking of his evolving, yet unevolved self.

Good thoughts and actions can never produce bad results; bad thoughts and actions can never produce good results. This is but saying that nothing can come from corn but corn, nothing from nettles but nettles. Men understand this law in the natural world, and work with it; but few understand it in the mental and moral world (though its operation there is just as simple and undeviating), and they, therefore, do not co-operate with it.

Suffering is *always* the effect of wrong thought in some direction. It is an indication that the individual is out of harmony with himself, with the Law of his being. The sole and supreme use of suffering is to purify, to burn out all that is useless and impure. Suffering ceases for him who is pure. There could be no object in burning gold after the dross had been removed, and a perfectly pure and enlightened being could not suffer.

ON CIRCUMSTANCES

The circumstances which a man encounters with suffering are the result of his own mental inharmony. The circumstances which a man encounters with blessedness are the result of his own mental harmony. Blessedness, not material possessions, is the measure of right thought; wretchedness, not lack of material possessions, is the measure of wrong thought. A man may be cursed and rich; he may be blessed and poor. Blessedness and riches are only joined together when the riches are rightly and wisely used; and the poor man only descends into wretchedness when he regards his lot as a burden unjustly imposed.

Indigence and indulgence are the two extremes of wretchedness. They are both equally unnatural and the result of mental disorder. A man is not rightly conditioned until he is a happy, healthy, and prosperous being; and happiness, health, and prosperity are the result of a harmonious adjustment of the inner with the outer, of the man with his surroundings.

A man only begins to be a man when he ceases to whine and revile, and commences to search for the hidden justice which regulates his life. And as he adapts his mind to that regulating factor, he ceases to accuse others as the cause of his condition, and builds himself up in strong and noble thoughts; ceases to kick against circumstances, but begins to *use* them as aids to his more rapid progress, and as a means of discovering the hidden powers and possibilities within himself.

Law, not confusion, is the dominating principle in the universe; justice, not injustice, is the soul and substance of life; and righteousness, not corruption, is the moulding and moving force in the spiritual government of the world. This being so, man has but to right himself to find that the universe is right; and during the process of putting himself right, he will find that as he alters his thoughts towards things and other people, things and other people will alter towards him.

The proof of this truth is in every person, and it therefore admits of easy investigation by systematic introspection and self-analysis. Let a man radi-

cally alter his thoughts, and he will be
astonished at the rapid transformation
it will effect in the material conditions
of his life. Men imagine that thought
can be kept secret, but it cannot; it
rapidly crystallizes into habit, and
habit solidifies into circumstance.
Bestial thoughts crystallize into habits
of drunkenness and sensuality, which
solidify into circumstances of destitu-
tion and disease: impure thoughts of
every kind crystallize into enervating
and confusing habits, which solidify
into distracting and adverse circumstances: thoughts of fear, doubt, and
indecision crystallize into weak, unmanly, and irresolute habits, which
solidify into circumstances of failure,
indigence, and slavish dependence:

34

lazy thoughts crystallize into habits of uncleanliness and dishonesty, which solidify into circumstances of foulness and beggary: hateful and condemnatory thoughts crystallize into habits of accusation and violence, which solidify into circumstances of injury and persecution: selfish thoughts of all kinds crystallize into habits of self-seeking, which solidify into circumstances more or less distressing. On the other hand, beautiful thoughts of all kinds crystallize into habits of grace and kindliness, which solidify into genial and sunny circumstances: pure thoughts crystallize into habits of temperance and self-control, which solidify into circumstances of repose and peace: thoughts of courage, self-

AS A MAN THINKETH

reliance, and decision crystallize into manly habits, which solidify into circumstances of success, plenty, and freedom: energetic thoughts crystallize into habits of cleanliness and industry, which solidify into circumstances of pleasantness: gentle and forgiving thoughts crystallize into habits of gentleness, which solidify into protective and preservative circumstances: loving and unselfish thoughts crystallize into habits of self-forgetfulness for others, which solidify into circumstances of sure and abiding prosperity and true riches.

A particular train of thought persisted in, be it good or bad, cannot fail to produce its results on the character and circumstances. A man cannot *directly* choose his circumstances, but he can choose his thoughts, and so indirectly, yet surely, shape his circumstances.

Nature helps every man to the gratification of the thoughts which he most encourages, and opportunities are presented which will most speedily bring to the surface both the good and evil thoughts.

Let a man cease from his sinful thoughts, and all the world will soften towards him, and be ready to help him; let him put away his weakly and sickly thoughts, and lo! opportunities will spring up on every hand to aid his strong resolves; let him encourage good thoughts, and no hard fate shall bind him down to wretchedness and shame. The world is your kaleido-scope, and the varying combinations of colors which at every succeeding moment it presents to you are the exquisitely adjusted pictures of your ever-moving thoughts.

"You will be what you will to be;
    Let failure find its false content
    In that poor word, 'environment,'
But spirit scorns it, and is free.

"It masters time, it conquers space;
    It cows that boastful trickster, Chance,
    And bids the tyrant Circumstance
Uncrown, and fill a servant's place.

"The human Will, that force unseen,
    The offspring of a deathless Soul,
    Can hew a way to any goal,
Though walls of granite intervene.

"Be not impatient in delay,
    But wait as one who understands;
    When spirit rises and commands,
The gods are ready to obey."

EFFECT OF THOUGHT
ON HEALTH AND THE BODY

THE body is the servant of the mind. It obeys the operations of the mind, whether they be deliberately chosen or automatically expressed. At the bidding of unlawful thoughts the body sinks rapidly into disease and decay; at the command of glad and beautiful thoughts it becomes clothed with youthfulness and beauty.

Disease and health, like circumstances, are rooted in thought. Sickly thoughts will express themselves

39

through a sickly body. Thoughts of fear have been known to kill a man as speedily as a bullet, and they are continually killing thousands of people just as surely though less rapidly. The people who live in fear of disease are the people who get it. Anxiety quickly demoralizes the whole body, and lays it open to the entrance of disease; while impure thoughts, even if not physically indulged, will soon shatter the nervous system.

Strong, pure, and happy thoughts build up the body in vigour and grace. The body is a delicate and plastic instrument, which responds readily to the thoughts by which it is impressed, and habits of thought will produce their own effects, good or bad, upon it.

Men will continue to have impure and poisoned blood so long as they propagate unclean thoughts. Out of a clean heart comes a clean life and a clean body. Out of a defiled mind proceeds a defiled life and a corrupt body. Thought is the fount of action, life, and manifestation; make the fountain pure, and all will be pure.

Change of diet will not help a man who will not change his thoughts. When a man makes his thoughts pure, he no longer desires impure food.

Clean thoughts make clean habits. The so-called saint who does not wash his body is not a saint. He who has strengthened and purified his thoughts does not need to consider the malevolent microbe.

If you would perfect your body,
guard your mind. If you would re-
new your body, beautify your mind.
Thoughts of malice, envy, disappoint-
ment, despondency, rob the body of
its health and grace. A sour face does
not come by chance; it is made by
sour thoughts. Wrinkles that mar
are drawn by folly, passion, pride.

I know a woman of ninety-six who
has the bright, innocent face of a girl.
I know a man well under middle age
whose face is drawn into inharmoni-
ous contours. The one is the result of
a sweet and sunny disposition; the
other is the outcome of passion and
discontent.

As you cannot have a sweet and
wholesome abode unless you admit

the air and sunshine freely into your rooms, so a strong body and a bright, happy, or serene countenance can only result from the free admittance into the mind of thoughts of joy and goodwill and serenity.

On the faces of the aged there are wrinkles made by sympathy; others by strong and pure thought, and others are carved by passion: who cannot distinguish them? With those who have lived righteously, age is calm, peaceful, and softly mellowed, like the setting sun. I have recently seen a philosopher on his death-bed. He was not old except in years. He died as sweetly and peacefully as he had lived.

There is no physician like cheerful

thought for dissipating the ills of the body: there is no comforter to compare with goodwill for dispersing the shadows of grief and sorrow. To live continually in thoughts of ill-will, cynicism, suspicion, and envy, is to be confined in a selfmade prisonhole. But to think well of all, to be cheerful with all, to patiently learn to find the good in all—such unselfish thoughts are the very portals of heaven; and to dwell day by day in thoughts of peace toward every creature will bring abounding peace to their possessor.

THOUGHT AND PURPOSE

UNTIL thought is linked with purpose there is no intelligent accomplishment. With the majority the barque of thought is allowed to "drift" upon the ocean of life. Aimlessness is a vice, and such drifting must not continue for him who would steer clear of catastrophe and destruction.

They who have no central purpose in their life fall an easy prey to petty worries, fears, troubles, and self-pityings, all of which are indications of weakness, which lead, just as surely as deliberately planned sins (though by a different route), to failure, unhappiness, and loss, for weakness cannot persist in a power-evolving universe.

A man should conceive of a legitimate purpose in his heart, and set out to accomplish it. He should make this purpose the centralizing point of his thoughts. It may take the form of a spiritual ideal, or it may be a worldly object, according to his nature at the time being; but whichever it is, he should steadily focus his thought-forces upon the object which he has set before him. He should make this purpose his supreme duty, and should devote himself to its attainment, not allowing his thoughts to wander away into ephemeral fancies, longings, and imaginings. This is the royal road to self-control and true concentration of thought. Even if he fails again and again to accomplish his purpose (as he necessarily must until weakness is overcome), the *strength of character gained* will be the measure of his *true* success, and this will form a new starting-point for future power and triumph.

Those who are not prepared for the apprehension of a *great* purpose, should fix the thoughts upon the faultless performance of their duty, no matter how insignificent their task may appear. Only in this way can the thoughts be gathered and focussed, and resolution and energy be developed, which being done, there is nothing which may not be accomplished.

The weakest soul, knowing its own weakness, and believing this truth—*that strength can only be developed by effort and practice*—will, thus believing, at once begin to exert itself, and, adding effort to effort, patience to patience, and strength to strength, will never cease to develop, and will at last grow divinely strong.

As the physically weak man can make himself strong by careful and patient training, so the man of weak thoughts can make them strong by exercising himself in right thinking.

To put away aimlessness and weakness, and to begin to think with purpose, is to enter the ranks of those strong ones who only recognize failure as one of the pathways to attainment; who make all conditions serve them, and who think strongly, attempt fearlessly, and accomplish masterfully.

Having conceived of his purpose, a man should mark out a *straight* pathway to its achievement, looking neither to the right nor the left. Doubts and fears should be rigorously excluded; they are disintegrating elements which break up the straight line of effort, rendering it crooked, ineffectual, useless. Thoughts of doubt and fear never accomplish anything, and never can. They always lead to failure. Purpose, energy, power to do, and all strong thoughts cease when doubt and fear creep in.

The will to do springs from the knowledge that we *can* do. Doubt and fear are the great enemies of knowledge, and he who encourages them, who does not slay them, thwarts himself at every step.

He who has conquered doubt and fear has conquered failure. His every thought is allied with power, and all difficulties are bravely met and wisely overcome. His purposes are seasonably planted, and they bloom and bring forth fruit which does not fall prematurely to the ground.

Thought allied fearlessly to purpose becomes creative force: he who *knows* this is ready to become something higher and stronger than a mere bundle of wavering thoughts and fluctuating sensations; he who *does* this has become the conscious and intelligent wielder of his mental powers.

THE THOUGHT-FACTOR
IN ACHIEVEMENT

ALL that a man achieves and all that he fails to achieve is the direct result of his own thoughts. In a justly ordered universe, where loss of equipoise would mean total destruction, individual responsibility must be absolute. A man's weakness and strength, purity and impurity, are his own, and not another man's; they are brought about by himself, and not by another; and they can only be altered by himself, never by another.

His condition is also his own, and not another man's. His suffering and his happiness are evolved from within. As he thinks, so he is; as he continues to think, so he remains.

A strong man cannot help a weaker unless that weaker is *willing* to be helped, and even then the weak man must become strong of himself; he must, by his own efforts, develop the strength which he admires in another. None but himself can alter his condition.

It has been usual for men to think and to say, "Many men are slaves because one is an oppressor; let us hate the oppressor." Now, however, there is amongst an increasing few a tendency to reverse this judgment, and to say, "One man is an oppressor because many are slaves; let us despise the slaves." The truth is that oppressor and slave are co-operators in ignorance, and, while seeming to afflict each other, are in reality afflicting themselves. A perfect Knowledge perceives the action of law in the weakness of the oppressed and the misapplied power of the oppressor; a perfect Love, seeing the suffering which both states entail, condemns neither; a perfect Compassion embraces both oppressor and oppressed.

He who has conquered weakness, and has put away all selfish thoughts, belongs neither to oppressor nor oppressed. He is free.

A man can only rise, conquer, and

achieve by lifting up his thoughts. He can only remain weak, and abject, and miserable by refusing to lift up his thoughts.

Before a man can achieve anything, even in worldy things, he must lift his thoughts above slavish animal indulgence. He may not, in order to succeed, give up *all* animality and selfishness, by any means; but a portion of it must, at least, be sacrificed. A man whose first thought is bestial indulgence could neither think clearly nor plan methodically; he could not find and develop his latent resources, and would fail in any undertaking. Not having commenced manfully to control his thoughts, he is not in a position to control affairs and to adopt serious responsibilities. He is not fit to act independently and stand alone. But he is limited only by the thoughts which he chooses.

There can be no progress, no achievement without sacrifice, and a man's worldly success will be in the measure that he sacrifices his confused animal thoughts, and fixes his mind on the development of his plans, and the strengthening of his resolution and self-reliance. And the higher he lifts his thoughts, the more manly, upright, and righteous he becomes, the greater will be his success, the more blessed and enduring will be his achievements.

The universe does not favour the greedy, the dishonest, the vicious, although on the mere surface it may sometimes appear to do so; it helps the honest, the magnanimous, the virtuous. All the great Teachers of the ages have declared this in varying forms, and to prove and know it a man has but to persist in making himself more and more virtuous by lifting up his thoughts.

Intellectual achievements are the result of thought consecrated to the search for knowledge, or for the beautiful and true in life and nature. Such achievements may be sometimes connected with vanity and ambition, but they are not the outcome of those characteristics; they are the natural outgrowth of long and arduous effort, and of pure and unselfish thoughts.

Spiritual achievements are the con-

summation of holy aspirations. He
who lives constantly in the conception
of noble and lofty thoughts, who
dwells upon all that is pure and unselfish, will, as surely as the sun
reaches its zenith and the moon its
full, become wise and noble in character, and rise into a position of influence and blessedness.

Achievement, of whatever kind, is
the crown of effort, the diadem of
thought. By the aid of self-control,
resolution, purity, righteousness, and
well-directed thought a man ascends;
by the aid of animality, indolence, impurity, corruption, and confusion of
thought a man descends.

A man may rise to high success in
the world, and even to lofty altitudes

in the spiritual realm, and again descend into weakness and wretchedness by allowing arrogant, selfish, and corrupt thoughts to take possession of him.

Victories attained by right thought can only be maintained by watchfulness. Many give way when success is assured, and rapidly fall back into failure.

All achievements, whether in the business, intellectual, or spiritual world, are the result of definitely directed thought, are governed by the same law and are of the same method; the only difference lies in *the object of attainment.*

He who would accomplish little must sacrifice little; he who would achieve much must sacrifice much; he who would attain highly must sacrifice greatly.

VISIONS AND IDEALS

THE dreamers are the saviours of the world. As the visible world is sustained by the invisible, so men, through all their trials and sins and sordid vocations, are nourished by the beautiful visions of their solitary dreamers. Humanity cannot forget its dreamers; it cannot let their ideals fade and die; it lives in them; it knows them as the *realities* which it shall one day see and know.

Composer, sculptor, painter, poet, prophet, sage, these are the makers of the after-world, the achitects of heaven. The world is beautiful because they have lived; without them, laboring humanity would perish.

He who cherishes a beautiful vision, a lofty ideal in his heart, will one day realize it. Columbus cherished a vision of another world, and he discovered it; Copernicus fostered the vision of a multiplicity of worlds and a wider universe, and he revealed it; Buddha beheld the vision of a spiritual world of stainless beauty and perfect peace, and he entered into it.

Cherish your visions; cherish your ideals; cherish the music that stirs in your heart, the beauty that forms in your mind, the loveliness that drapes your purest thoughts, for out of them will grow all delightful conditions, all heavenly environment; of these, if you but remain true to them, your world will at last be built.

To desire is to obtain; to aspire is to achieve. Shall man's basest desires receive the fullest measure of gratification, and his purest aspirations starve for lack of sustenance? Such is not the Law: such a condition of things can never obtain: "Ask and receive."

Dream lofty dreams, and as you dream, so shall you become. Your Vision is the promise of what you shall one day be; your Ideal is the prophecy of what you shall at last unveil.

The greatest achievement was at

63

first and for a time a dream. The oak
sleeps in the acorn; the bird waits in
the egg; and in the highest vision of
the soul a waking angel stirs. Dreams
are the seedlings of realities.

Your circumstances may be uncon-
genial, but they shall not long remain
so if you but perceive an Ideal and
strive to reach it. You cannot travel
within and stand still *without*. Here is
a youth hard pressed by poverty and
labor; confined long hours in an un-
healthy workshop; unschooled, and
lacking all the arts of refinement.
But he dreams of better things; he
thinks of intelligence, of refinement, of
grace and beauty. He conceives of,
mentally builds up, an ideal condition
of life; the vision of a wider liberty and

a larger scope takes possession of him; unrest urges him to action, and he utilizes all his spare time and means, small though they are, to the development of his latent powers and resources. Very soon so altered has his mind become that the workshop can no longer hold him. It has become so out of harmony with his mentality that it falls out of his life as a garment is cast aside, and, with the growth of opportunities which fit the scope of his expanding powers, he passes out of it forever. Years later we see this youth as a full-grown man. We find him a master of certain forces of the mind which he wields with world-wide influence and almost unequalled power. In his hands he holds the cords of gigantic responsibilities; he speaks, and lo! lives are changed; men and women hang upon his words and re-mould their characters, and, sunlike, be becomes the fixed and luminous center around which innumerable des-tinies revolve. He has realized the Vision of his youth. He has become one with his Ideal.

And you, too, youthful reader, will realize the Vision (not the idle wish) of your heart, be it base or beautiful, or a mixture of both, for you will al-ways gravitate toward that which you, secretly, most love. Into your hands will be placed the exact re-sults of your own thoughts; you will receive that which you earn; no more, no less. Whatever your present en-

vironment may be, you will fall, remain, or rise with your thoughts, your
Vision, your Ideal. You will become
as small as your controlling desire; as
great as your dominant aspiration:
in the beautiful words of Stanton
Kirkham Davis, "You may be keeping accounts, and presently you shall
walk out of the door that for so long
has seemed to you the barrier of your
ideals, and shall find yourself before
an audience—the pen still behind
your ear, the inkstains on your fingers
—and then and there shall pour out
the torrent of your inspiration. You
may be driving sheep, and you shall
wander to the city—bucolic and open-
mouthed; shall wander under the in-
trepid guidance of the spirit into the

studio of the master, and after a time he shall say, 'I have nothing more to teach you.' And now you have become the master, who did so recently dream of great things while driving sheep. You shall lay down the saw and the plane to take upon yourself the regeneration of the world."

The thoughtless, the ignorant, and the indolent, seeing only the apparent effects of things and not the things themselves, talk of luck, of fortune, and chance. Seeing a man grow rich, they say, "How lucky he is!" Observing another become intellectual, they exclaim, "How highly favoured he is!" And noting the saintly character and wide influence of another, they remark, "How chance aids him at every turn!" They do not see the trials and failures and struggles which these men have voluntarily encountered in order to gain their experience; have no knowledge of the sacrifices they have made, of the undaunted efforts they have put forth, of the faith they have exercised, that they might overcome the apparently insurmountable, and realize the Vision of their heart. They do not know the darkness and the heartaches; they only see the light and joy, and call it "luck"; do not see the long and arduous journey, but only behold the pleasant goal, and call it "good fortune"; do not understand the process, but only perceive the result, and call it "chance."

In all human affairs there are *efforts*, and there are *results*, and the strength of the effort is the measure of the result. Chance is not. "Gifts," powers, material, intellectual, and spiritual possessions are the fruits of effort; they are thoughts completed, objects accomplished, visions realized.

The Vision that you glorify in your mind, the Ideal that you enthrone in your heart—this you will build your life by, this you will become.

SERENITY

CALMNESS of mind is one of the beautiful jewels of wisdom. It is the result of long and patient effort in self-control. Its presence is an indication of ripened experience, and of a more than ordinary knowledge of the laws and operations of thought.

A man becomes calm in the measure that he understands himself as a thought-evolved being, for such knowledge necessitates the understanding of others as the result of thought, and as he develops a right understanding,

71

and sees more and more clearly the internal relations of things by the action of cause and effect, he ceases to fuss and fume and worry and grieve, and remains poised, steadfast, serene.

The calm man, having learned how to govern himself, knows how to adapt himself to others; and they, in turn, reverence his spiritual strength, and feel that they can learn of him and rely upon him. The more tranquil a man becomes, the greater is his success, his influence, his power for good. Even the ordinary trader will find his business prosperity increase as he develops a greater self-control and equanimity, for people will always prefer to deal with a man whose demeanour is strongly equable.

SERENITY

The strong, calm man is always loved and revered. He is like a shade-giving tree in a thirsty land, or a sheltering rock in a storm. "Who does not love a tranquil heart, a sweet-tempered, balanced life? It does not matter whether it rains or shines, or what changes come to those possessing these blessings, for they are always sweet, serene, and calm. That exquisite poise of character which we call serenity is the last lesson of culture; it is the flowering of life, the fruitage of the soul. It is precious as wisdom, more to be desired than gold—yea, than even fine gold. How insignificant mere money-seeking looks in comparison with a serene life—a life that dwells in the ocean of Truth, beneath the waves, beyond the reach of tempests, in the Eternal Calm!

"How many people we know who sour their lives, who ruin all that is sweet and beautiful by explosive tempers, who destroy their poise of character, and make bad blood! It is a question whether the great majority of people do not ruin their lives and mar their happiness by lack of self-control. How few people we meet in life who are well-balanced, who have that exquisite poise which is characteristic of the finished character!"

Yes, humanity surges with uncontrolled passion, is tumultuous with ungoverned grief, is blown about by anxiety and doubt. Only the wise man, only he whose thoughts are controlled and purified, makes the winds and the storms of the soul obey him.

Tempest-tossed souls, wherever ye may be, under whatsoever conditions ye may live, know this—in the ocean of life the isles of Blessedness are smiling, and the sunny shore of your ideal awaits your coming. Keep your hand firmly upon the helm of thought. In the barque of your soul reclines the commanding Master; He does but sleep; wake Him. Self-control is strength; Right Thought is mastery; Calmness is power. Say unto your heart, "Peace, be still!"

Sun Books
Sun Publishing
Supplement B-5

MOTIVATIONAL BOOKS
FROM THESE FINE AUTHORS

- **James Allen**
- **Lily L. Allen (Mrs. James Allen)**
- **Christian D. Larson**
- **Orison Swett Marden**
- **Ralph Waldo Trine**

JAMES ALLEN

ABOVE LIFE'S TURMOIL by James Allen. True Happiness, The Immortal Man, The Overcoming of Self, The Uses of Temptation, The Man of Integrity, Discrimination, Belief, The Basis of Action, The Belief that Saves, Thought and Action, Your Mental Attitude, Sowing and Reaping, The Reign of Law, The Supreme Justice, The Use of Reason, Self-Discipline, Resolution, The Glorious Conquest, Contentment in Activity, The Temple of Brotherhood, Pleasant Pastures of Peace. 163 pgs. 5x8. Pbk. ISBN: 0-89540-203-3.

ALL THESE THINGS ADDED by James Allen. Entering the Kingdom, The Soul's Great Need, The Competitive Laws and the Law of Love, The Finding of a Principle, At Rest in the Kingdom, The Heavenly Life, The Divine Center, The Eternal Now, The "Original Simplicity", The Unfailing Wisdom, The Might of Meekness, The Righteous Man, Perfect Love, Greatness and Goodness, and Heaven in the Heart. 192 pgs. 5x8. Pbk. ISBN: 0-89540-129-0.

AS A MAN THINKETH by James Allen. Thought and Character, Effect of Thought on Circumstances, Effect of Thought on Health and the Body, Thought and Purpose, The Thought-Factor in Achievement, Visions and Ideals, Serenity. 88 pgs. 5x8. Pbk. ISBN: 0-89540-136-3.

BYWAYS OF BLESSEDNESS by James Allen. Right Beginnings, Small Tasks and Duties, Transcending Difficulties and Perplexities, Burden-Dropping, Hidden Sacrifices, Sympathy, Forgiveness, Seeing No Evil,

Abiding Joy, Silentness, Solitude, Standing Alone, Understanding the Simple Laws of Life, Happy Endings. 202 pgs. 5x8. Pbk. ISBN: 0-89540-202-5.

THE DIVINE COMPANION by James Allen. Truth as Awakener, Truth as Protector, Of Discipline and Purification, Of Purity of Heart, The First Prophecy - Called Awakening, The Fifth Prophecy - Called Transition, The Second Exhortation - Concerning Humility, Instruction Concerning the Great Reality, Discourse Concerning The Way of Truth, Self-Restraint, Etc. 152 pgs. 5x8. Pbk. ISBN: 0-89540-329-3.

EIGHT PILLARS OF PROSPERITY by James Allen. Discussion on Energy, Economy, Integrity, Systems, Sympathy, Sincerity, Impartiality, Self-reliance, and the Temple of Prosperity. 233 pgs. 5x8. Pbk. ISBN: 0-89540-201-7.

ENTERING THE KINGDOM by James Allen. The Soul's Great Need, The Competitive Laws and the Laws of Love, The Finding of a Principle, At Rest in the Kingdom, And All Things Added. 82 pgs. 5x8. Pbk. ISBN: 0-89540-226-2.

FOUNDATION STONES TO HAPPINESS AND SUCCESS by James Allen. Right Principles, Sound Methods, True Actions, True Speech, Equal Mindedness, Good Results. 53 pgs. 5x8. Pbk. ISBN: 0-89540-327-7.

FROM PASSION TO PEACE by James Allen. Passion, Aspiration, Temptation, Transmutation, Transcendence, Beatitude, Peace. 64 pgs. 5x8. Pbk. ISBN: 0-89540-077-4.

FROM POVERTY TO POWER by James Allen. Two books in one: The Path to Prosperity including World a Reflex of Mental States, The Way Out of Undesirable Conditions, Silent Power of Thought, Controlling and Directing One's Forces, The Secret of Health, Success, and Power, Etc. and The Way of Peace including Power of Meditation, The Two Masters, Self and Truth, The Acquirement of Spiritual Power, Realization of Selfless Love, Entering into the Infinite, Perfect Peace, Etc. 184 pgs. 5x8. Pbk. ISBN: 0-89540-061-8.

THE HEAVENLY LIFE by James Allen. The Divine Center, The Eternal Now, The "Original Simplicity," The Unfailing Wisdom, The Might of Meekness, The Righteous Man, Perfect Love, Perfect Freedom, Greatness and Goodness, Heaven in the Heart.84 pgs. 5x8. Pbk. ISBN:0-89540-227-0.

THE LIFE TRIUMPHANT by James Allen. Faith and Courage, Manliness and Sincerity, Energy and Power, Self-Control and Happiness, Simplicity and Freedom, Right-Thinking and Repose, Calmness and Resource, Insight and Nobility, Man and the Master, and Knowledge and Victory. 114 pgs. 5x8. Pbk. ISBN: 0-89540-125-8.

LIGHT ON LIFE'S DIFFICULTIES by James Allen. The Light that Leads to Perfect Peace, The Law of Cause and Effect in Human Life, Values - Spiritual and Material, Adherence to Principle, The Sacrifice of The Self, The Management of the Mind, Self-Control, Acts and Their Consequences, The Way of Wisdom, The Blessing and Dignity of Work, Good Manner and Refinement, Diversity of Creeds, War and Peace, The Brotherhood of Man, Life's Sorrows, Life's Change, Etc. 137 pgs. 5x8. Pbk. ISBN: 0-89540-217-3.

MAN: KING OF MIND, BODY AND CIRCUMSTANCE by James Allen. The Inner World of Thoughts, The Outer World of Things, Habit: Its Slavery and Its Freedom, Bodily Conditions, Poverty, Man's Spiritual Dominion, Conquest. 55 pgs. 5x8. Pbk. ISBN: 0-89540-212-2.

THE MASTERY OF DESTINY by James Allen. Deeds, Character, and Destiny, The Science of Self- Control, Cause and Effect in Human Conduct, Training of the Will, Thoroughness, Mind-Building and Life-Building, Cultivation of Concentration, Practice of Meditation, Power of Purpose, Joy of Accomplishment. 120 pgs. 5x8. Pbk. ISBN: 0-89540-209-2.

MEDITATIONS - A YEAR BOOK by James Allen. "James Allen may truly be called the Prophet of Meditation. In an age of strife, hurry, religious controversy, heated arguments, ritual and ceremony, he came with his message of Meditation, calling men away from the din and strife of tongues into the peaceful paths of stillness within their own souls, where 'the Light that lighteth every man that cometh into the world' ever burns steadily and surely for all who will turn their weary eyes from the strife without to the quiet within." Contains two inspiring quotations and a brief commentary for each day of the year. 366 pgs. 5x8. Pbk. ISBN: 0-89540-192-4.

MEN AND SYSTEMS by James Allen. Men and Systems, Work, Wages, and Well-Being, The Survival of the Fittest as Divine Law, Justice in Evil, Justice and Love, Self-Protection - Animal, Human, and Divine, Aviation and the New Consciousness, The New Courage. 149 pgs. 5x8. Pbk. ISBN: 0- 89540-326-9.

MORNING AND EVENING THOUGHTS by James Allen. Contains a separate and brief paragraph for each morning and evening of the month. 71 pgs. 5x8. Pbk. ISBN: 0-89540-137-1.

OUT FROM THE HEART by James Allen. The Heart and the Life, The Nature of Power of Mind, Formation of Habit, Doing and Knowing, First Steps in the Higher Life, Mental Conditions and Their Effects, Exhortation. 54 pgs. 5x8. Pbk. ISBN: 0-89540-228-9.

THE PATH TO PROSPERITY by James Allen. The Lesson of Evil, The World a Reflex of Mental States, The Way Out of Undesirable Conditions,

The Silent Power of Thought: Controlling and Directing One's Forces, The Secret of Health Success and Power, The Secret of Abounding Happiness, The Realization of Prosperity. 88 pgs. 5x8. Pbk. ISBN: 0-89540-403-6.

POEMS OF PEACE, Including The Lyrical Dramatic Poem EOLAUS by James Allen. 38 Poems. 84 pgs. Pbk. ISBN: 0-89540-429-X.

THE SHINING GATEWAY by James Allen. The Shining Gateway of Meditation, Temptation, Regeneration, Actions and Motives, Morality and Religion, Memory, Repetition and Habit, Words and Wisdom, Truth Made Manifest, Spiritual Humility, Spiritual Strength, Etc. 58 pgs. 5x8. Pbk. ISBN: 0-89540-328-5.

THROUGH THE GATE OF GOOD by James Allen. The Gate and the Way, The Law and the Prophets, The Yoke and the Burden, The Word and the Doer, The Vine and the Branches, Salvation this Day. 66 pgs. 5x8. Pbk. ISBN: 0-89540-216-5.

THE WAY OF PEACE by James Allen. The Power of Meditation, The Two Masters: Self and Truth, The Acquirement of Spiritual Power, The Realization of Selfless Love, Entering into the Infinite, Saints, Sages, and Saviors, The Law of Service, The Realization of Perfect Peace. 113 pgs. 5x8. Pbk. ISBN: 0-89540-229-7.

Lily L. Allen (Mrs. James Allen)

THE BRYNGOLEU COOKERY BOOK. A Humanitarian Household Guide by Lily L. Allen. Breakfast Menus for One Week, Home, Luncheon Menus, The Cuisine of the Compassionate, Dinner Menus, Hints to Housewives, Soups, Sauces, Gravies, Sweets, Bread and Cakes, Etc. 66 pgs. 5x8. Pbk. ISBN: 0-89540-456-7.

CLUES TO THE TREASURES OF LIFE by Lily L. Allen. Chapters include: Clues to Life's Treasures, Clues to the Secret of Health, The Greatest of All Clues, Clues to the Abundant Life, Clues to the Glorious Destination of Man, Finding the Deathless Life, The Law of Attraction, The Will of God Concerning Man, Clues for Everyday Life, Etc. 83 pgs. 5x8. Pbk. ISBN: 0-89540-451-6. (ISBN-13: 978-0-89540-451-0).

ELEMENTS OF SUCCESS by Lily L. Allen. The Fine Art of Living, The Essential Ideal, The Survival of the Fittest, Thought - The Greatest Element in Success, Difficulties, Drawbacks, The Equal Mind, The Success Habit, Climbing to Success, Etc. 136 pgs. 5x8. Pbk. ISBN: 0-89540-446-X.

GUIDE TO A HEALTHY, HAPPY, AND HUMANE LIFE by Lily L. Allen. 130 pgs. 5x8. Pbk. ISBN: 0-89540-460-5.

HEALING FOR ALL OUR ILLS by Lily L. Allen. Clearing the Mind, Reversing the Thoughts, Self-Treatment, We Are in Heaven Now, The Use of Denials, The Use of Affirmations, Healing Treatments, Mixed-Thinking, Thinking of Others, The Need of Patience, The Power of Words, Perfect Health, The Abundant Life, The Ideal is Always the Real, The Vision of the Healer, Etc. 79 pgs. 5x8. Pbk. ISBN: 0-89540-453-2.

HOW TO GO INTO THE SILENCE by Lily L. Allen. Chapters include: Going Into the Silence, How to Enter the Silence, Why We Go Into the Silence, Waiting In the Silence. 23 pgs. 5x8. Pbk. ISBN: 0-89540-452-4.

IN THE GARDEN OF SILENCE by Lily L. Allen. Told in the Twilight, Immortality, Opportunity, Penelope, My Gold!, Afterward, Unbroken Alabaster. 59 pgs. 5x8. Pbk. ISBN: 0-89540-420-6.

THE KNOWLEDGE THAT BRINGS PEACE by Lily L. Allen. Chapters include: The Knowledge That Brings Peace, The Law of the Increase of All Good, A New Order of Thought, A New Method of Thinking. 47 pgs. 5x8. Pbk. ISBN: 0-89540-455-9.

THE LIFE OF POWER AND DOMINION by Lily L. Allen. The Outlook, What Man Is, The One Creator, Affirming the Truth, The Law of Growth, The Perfect Harmony, The Outpouring of All Good, Believing and Receiving, The Life of Power and Dominion, Work: The Glory of Life, Inheritors of All Good. 64 pgs. 5x8. Pbk. ISBN: 0-89540-449-4.

LIFE'S INSPIRATIONS by Lily L. Allen. Unseen Forces, Beauty, Nature, Friendship, Smiles, Work, Companionship and Solitude, Sorrow, Thinking to Inspire, What We Call Death, Life's Greatest Inspiration, Etc. 167 pgs. 5x8. Pbk. ISBN: 0-89540-457-5. (ISBN-13: 978-0-89540-457-2).

THE MEANING AND USE OF THE SILENCE by Lily L. Allen. The True Knowledge of Prayer, The Prayer That is Always Answered, The Realisation of Our Sonship, The Soul's Trysting Place and Time, The Silence for Meditation, Why the Silence is Necessary, The Power of the Silence in the Day's Work, Perfect Rest and Confidence Through the Silence. 55 pgs. 5x8. Pbk. ISBN: 0-89540-454-0.

THE MIGHT OF MIND by Lily L. Allen. Control of the Mind, Creative Power of Mind, Thought - The Alchemist, Desire or Aspiration, What Will Ye? The Influence of Thought on Environment, The Philosopher's Stone, "With All Thy Getting." 79 pgs. 5x8. Pbk. ISBN: 0-89540-443-5.

THE MINISTRY OF SILENT HELPERS by Lily L. Allen. The Ministry of Silent Helpers, The Divine Relationship and What It Implies, Seeing As God Sees, The Power of Right Thinking, The Master of My Fate, Seeking First the Kingdom. 87 pgs. 5x8. Pbk. ISBN: 0-89540-448-6.

ONE LIFE, ONE LAW, ONE LOVE by Lily L. Allen. The World Within, Inward Light, Becoming, Law of Love, Limitations, Taking Time to Think, Where Understanding Dwells. 57 pgs. Pbk. ISBN: 0-89540-445-1.

OUR CREATIVE IMAGINATION by Lily L. Allen. Imagination: What Is It?, The Law of Correspondences, The Eternal Now, The Eternal Memory, Mental Impressions, Divine Alchemy, Removing Mountains, The Eternal Good, The Pathway of the Conqueror. 50 pgs. 5x8. Pbk. ISBN: 0-89540-450-8. (ISBN-13: 978-0-89540-450-3).

OUR MENTAL CHILDREN by Lily L. Allen. Our Thought Children, Fear, Pride, Suspicion, Sincerity, Hope, The Beautiful, Some Simple Rules. 42 pgs. Pbk. ISBN: 0-89540-447-8.

PERSONALITY: ITS CULTIVATION AND POWER AND HOW TO ATTAIN by Lily L. Allen. Personality, Right Belief, Self-Knowledge, Intuition, Decision and Promptness, Self-Trust, Thoroughness, Manners, Physical Culture, Mental, Moral, and Spiritual Culture, Introspection, Emancipation, Self-Development, Self-Control and Mental Poise, Liberty, Transformation, Balance, Meditation and Concentration. 170 pgs. 5x8. Pbk. ISBN: 0-89540-218-1.

CHRISTIAN D. LARSON

BRAINS AND HOW TO GET THEM by Christian D. Larson. Building the Brain, Making Every Brain Cell Active, Principles in Brain Building, Practical Methods in Brain Building, Vital Secrets in Brain Building, Special Brain Development, The Inner Secret, The Finer Forces, Subjective Concentration, Principle of Concentration, Development of Business Ability, Accumulation and Increase, Individual Advancement, The Genius of Invention, The Musical Prodigy, Talent and Genius in Art, Talent and Genius in Literature, Vital Essentials In Brain Building. 233 pgs. 5x8. Pbk. ISBN 0-89540-382-X.

BUSINESS INSPIRATIONS by Christian D. Larson. Chapters include: Follow the High Vision, Inspiration Moves the World, This Will Mean Success, How We Gain Power, The Good Cheer Attitude, The Magic of Sincerity, It Pays to Look Well, The Full Positive Action, Virtues of Persistent Desire, Demand More of Yourself, What Makes Men Great, Giving Your Whole Self, Knowing How to Work, The Whole Mind in Action, Creating the Right Idea, The Will to Do More, etc. 163 pgs. 5x8. Pbk. ISBN: 0-89540-399-4.

THE HIDDEN SECRET by Christian D. Larson. There is a life within that has no limit; it is the life more abundant - the life that every awakened mind has sought with heart and soul; it is the life from which all great things proceed; the source of everything that has real value and high worth. 101 pgs. 5x8. Pbk. ISBN: 0-89540-404-4.

HOW GREAT MEN SUCCEED by Christian D. Larson. The man who succeeds is invariably impelled to press on and on by something within him that tells him he can... In the spirit of this conviction he proceeds with his eye singled upon the goal in view, gaining ground steadily and demonstrating every day, through actual results, that his conviction is based upon fact. 95 pgs. 5x8. Pbk. ISBN: 0-89540-398-6.

JUST BE GLAD by Christian D. Larson. For great is the power of sunshine, especially human sunshine. It can change anything, transform anything, remake anything, and cause anything to become as fair and beautiful as itself. 64 Pages. 5x8. Pbk. ISBN: 0-89540-441-9.

MASTERY OF FATE by Christian D. Larson. What man is, and what man does, determines in what conditions, circumstances, and environments he shall be placed. Since man can change both himself and his actions, he can determine what his fate is. 95 pgs. 5x8. Pbk. ISBN: 0-89540-383-8.

MASTERY OF SELF by Christian D. Larson. No power in man can do what it is created to do, and what it has the capacity to do, until it is directed by man himself; powers, elements, forces, and things are at the disposal of man; they can do only what he directs them to do; they respond only to his control, but before man can gain the power to master forces and things, he must gain the power to master himself. 87 pgs. 5x8. Pbk. ISBN: 0-89540-384-6.

NOTHING SUCCEEDS LIKE SUCCESS by Christian D. Larson. When we think of success, we usually think of the accumulation of wealth, but this can never be more than a small fragment of success, because success in reality signifies any form of attainment or achievement that is truly worth while. 80 pgs. 5x8. Pbk. ISBN: 0-89540-385-4.

ON THE HEIGHTS by Christian D. Larson. We are under the clear sky of Infinite Light, on the verge of the great beyond, on the border-land of the limitless, and every moment is an eternity of ecstasy divine. 74 pgs. 5x8. Pbk. ISBN: 0-89540-442-7.

PERFECT HEALTH by Christian D. Larson. To apply the principle of faith in the realization of perfect health, enter into the spirit of perfect health whenever you think of health. Live in the soul of health, or the real, interior life of health. 78 pgs. 5x8. Pbk. ISBN: 0-89540-397-8.

PRACTICAL SELF-HELP by Christian D. Larson. Chapters include: Lean to Help Yourself, What You Should Do, Changing Your Own World, The Successful Mental Attitude, Full Use of Ability and Power, The Control of Circumstance, Effective Use of Thought and Action, Vital Principles in Self-Help, Building Self-Confidence, Invincible Determination, Know What You Want, The Control of Things, There is

Always a Way, Actions That Produce Response, Directing the Forces of Life, The Most Helpful Principle Known Today, Etc! 223 pgs. 5x8. Pbk. ISBN: 0-89540-400-1.

THINKING FOR RESULTS by Christian D. Larson. That man can change himself, improve himself, recreate himself, control his environment, and master his own destiny is the conclusion of every mind that is wide-awake to the power of right thought in constructive action. In fact, it is the conviction of all such minds that man can do practically anything within the possibilities of the human domain when he knows how to think, and that he can secure almost any result desired when he learns how to think for results. 132 pgs. 5x8. Pbk. ISBN: 0-89540-381-1.

WHAT RIGHT THINKING WILL DO by Christian D. Larson. Whenever we think, we form a mental image of that about which we are thinking; or we may speak of it as a mental picture; and in the science of right thinking, the question is, what kind of mental pictures or images we shall form, because we understand the fact that every mental image becomes a pattern in the mind, and the creative energies of the mind will produce states, conditions, and qualities that correspond exactly with the mental image. 50 pgs. 5x8. Pbk. ISBN: 0-89540-386-2.

YOUR FORCES AND HOW TO USE THEM by Christian D. Larson. How We Govern the Forces We Possess, The Use of Mind in Practical Action, Training the Subconscious for Special Results, How Man Becomes What He Thinks, He Can Who Thinks He Can, How We Secure What We Persistently Desire, Concentration and the Power of Suggestion, The Development of the Will, The Building of a Great Mind, How Character Determines Constructive Action, The Creative Forces in Man, Imagination and the Master Mind, Etc. 331 pgs. 6x8. Pbk. ISBN 0-89540-380-3.

ORISON SWETT MARDEN

AMBITION AND SUCCESS by Orison Swett Marden. What is Ambition, The Satisfied Man, The Influence of Environment, Unworthy Ambitions, Ambition Knows No Age Limit, Make Your Life Count, Visualize Yourself in a Better Position, Thwarted Ambition, Why Don't You Begin? 75 pgs. 5x8. Pbk. ISBN: 0-89540-369-2.

BE GOOD TO YOURSELF by Orison Swett Marden. 322 pgs. 5x8. Pbk. ISBN: 0-89540-364-1.

CHARACTER - THE GRANDEST THING IN THE WORLD by Orison Swett Marden. A Grand Character, The Light Bearers, The Great-Hearted, Intrepidity of Spirit, "A Fragment of the Rock of Ages," Etc. 55 pgs. Pbk. ISBN: 0-89540-297-1.

CHEERFULNESS AS A LIFE POWER by Orison Swett Marden. Inspiration, Self-Help, Positive Thinking, Recovery, Business Etiquette. 79 pgs. 5x8. Pbk. ISBN: 0-89540-363-3.

CHOOSING A CAREER by Orison Swett Marden. 332 pgs. 5x8. Pbk. ISBN: 0-89540-412-5.

THE CONQUEST OF WORRY by Orison Swett Marden. 535 pgs. 5x8. Pbk. ISBN: 0-89540-396-X

EVERY MAN A KING, or Might in Mind Mastery by Orison Swett Marden. Steering Thought Prevents Life Wrecks, How Mind Rules the Body, Thought Causes Health and Disease, Overcoming Fear, Mastering our Moods, The Power of Cheerful Thinking, Affirmation Creates Power, How Thinking Brings Success, Building Character, The Power of Imagination, How to Control Thought, Etc. 240 pgs. 5x8. Pbk. ISBN: 0-89540-334-X.

EVERYBODY AHEAD OR GETTING THE MOST OUT OF LIFE by Orison Swett Marden. 535 pgs. 5x8. Pbk. ISBN: 0-89540-409-5.

THE EXCEPTIONAL EMPLOYEE by Orison Swett Marden. Inspiration, positive thinking, self-help, business. 202 pgs. 5x8 pgs. Pbk. ISBN: 0-89540-352-8.

GETTING ON by Orison Swett Marden. 325 pgs. 5x8. Pbk. ISBN: 0-89540-370-6.

GOOD MANNERS - A PASSPORT TO SUCCESS by Orison Swett Marden. 64 pgs. 5x8. Pbk. ISBN:0-89540-366-8.

HE CAN WHO THINKS HE CAN by Orison Swett Marden. He Can Who Thinks He Can, Getting Aroused, Education by Absorption, Freedom at Any Cost, What the World Owes to Dreamers, The Spirit in Which You Work, Responsibility Develops Power, Stand for Something, Happy, If Not, Why? Originality, Sizing Up People, Getting Away From Poverty, Etc. 245 pgs. 5x8. Pbk. ISBN: 0-89540-346-3.

THE HOUR OF OPPORTUNITY by Orison Swett Marden. The Hour of Opportunity: Are You Ready For It? Self-Made or Never Made, Do Not Wait for Opportunity, Self-Training, Do You Know a Good Thing When You See It? Every-Day Opportunities, The Executive Quality, What is My Right Place, "I Never Asked Anything About It," The Power of Adaptation, Focus Your Energies, Become a Specialist, The Inspiration of a Great Purpose, Etc. 72 pgs. 5x8. Pbk. ISBN: 0-89540-336-6.

HOW THEY SUCCEEDED - LIFE STORIES OF SUCCESSFUL MEN AND WOMEN TOLD BY THEMSELVES by Orison Swett Marden. Marshall Field, Alexander G. Bell, Helen Gould, Philip D.

Armour, Mary E. Proctor, John Wanamaker, Darius Ogden Mills, Lillian Nordica, John D. Rockefeller, Julia Ward Howe, Thomas A. Edison, Lew Wallace, Andrew Carnegie, John Burroughs, James Whitcomb Riley, Etc. 365 pgs. 5x8. Pbk. ISBN: 0-89540-345-5.

HOW TO SUCCEED or STEPPING STONES TO FAME AND FORTUNE by Orison Swett Marden. 332 pgs. 5x8. Pbk. ISBN: 0-89540-371-4.

HOW TO GET WHAT YOU WANT by Orison Swett Marden. How to Get What You Want, Discouragement a Disease, How to Cure It, The Force that Moves Mountains, Faith and Drugs, How to Find Oneself, How to Attract Prosperity, Heart-to-Heart Talks With Yourself, Etc. 331 pgs. 5x8. Pbk. ISBN: 0-89540-335-8.

AN IRON WILL by Orison Swett Marden. Training the Will, Mental Discipline, Conscious Power, Do You Believe in Yourself? Will Power in its Relation to Health and Disease, The Romance of Achievement Under Difficulties, Concentrated Energy, Staying Power, Persistent Purpose, Success Against Odds. 52 pgs. Pbk. ISBN: 0-89540-283-1.

THE JOYS OF LIVING OR LIVING TODAY IN THE HERE AND NOW by Orison Swett Marden. 403 pgs. 5x8. Pbk. ISBN: 0-89540-389-7.

LITTLE VISITS WITH GREAT AMERICANS. TWO VOLUME SET by Orison Swett Marden. 742 pgs. 5x8. Pbk. ISBN: 0-89540-374-9.

LITTLE VISITS WITH GREAT AMERICANS. VOL. II by Orison Swett Marden. 389 pgs. 5x8. Pbk. ISBN: 0-89540-373-0.

LITTLE VISITS WITH GREAT AMERICANS. VOL. I by Orison Swett Marden. 352 pgs. 5x8. Pbk. ISBN: 0-89540-372-2.

MAKING LIFE A MASTERPIECE by Orison Swett Marden. 329 pgs. 5x8. Pbk. ISBN: 0-89540-365-X.

THE MAKING OF A MAN by Orison Swett Marden. 307 pgs. 5x8. Pbk. ISBN: 0-89540-408-7.

MAKING YOURSELF by Orison Swett Marden. 320 pgs. 5x8. Pbk. ISBN: 0-89540-413-3.

THE MIRACLE OF RIGHT THOUGHT by Orison Swett Marden. Working for One Thing and Expecting Something Else, Expect Great Things of Yourself, Self-Encouragement by Self-Suggestion, Change the Thought - Change the Man, The Paralysis of Fear, Getting in Tune, A New Way of Bringing Up Children, Training for Longevity, As A Man Thinketh, Etc. 339 pgs. Pbk. ISBN: 0-89540-311-0.

NOT THE SALARY BUT THE OPPORTUNITY by Orison Swett Marden. 96 pgs. 5x8. Pbk. ISBN: 0-89540-410-9.

THE OPTIMISTIC LIFE by Orison Swett Marden. The Power of Amiability, The Inner Life as Related to Outward Beauty, The Value of Friends, The Cost of an Explosive Temper, Learn to Expect a Great Deal of Life, Mental Power, If You Can Talk Well, Brevity and Directness, What Distinguishes Work From Drudgery, Keeping Fit for Work, Mastering Moods, Business Integrity, Wresting Triumphant from Defeat, Freshness in Work, Don't Take Your Business Troubles Home, Let It Go, Etc! 316 pgs. 5x8. Pbk. ISBN: 0-89540-351-X.

PEACE, POWER, AND PLENTY by Orison Swett Marden. The Power of the Mind to Compel the Body, Poverty a Mental Disease, The Law of Opulence, Character-Building and Health-Building During Sleep, Health Through Right Thinking, Imagination and Health, How Suggestion Influences Health, Why Grow Old?, The Miracle of Self-Confidence, Self-Control vs the Explosive Passions, Good Cheer - God's Medicine, Etc. 323 pgs. 5x8. Pbk. ISBN: 0-89540-343-9.

THE POWER OF PERSONALITY by Orison Swett Marden. Inspiration, Self-Help, Positive Thinking, Recovery, Business Etiquette. 86 pgs. 5x8. Pbk. ISBN: 0-89540-362-5.

THE PROGRESSIVE BUSINESS MAN or How the Right Mental Attitude and Reciprocity are Revolutionizing Business by Orison Swett Marden. 166 pgs. 5x8. Pbk. ISBN: 0-89540-390-0.

PROSPERITY, HOW TO ATTRACT IT by Orison Swett Marden. 325 pgs. 5x8. Pbk. ISBN: 0-89540-392-7.

PUSHING TO THE FRONT VOL I by Orison Swett Marden. Opportunities Where You Are, Possibilities in Spare Time, How Poor Boys and Girls Go to College, Your Opportunity Confronts You, What Will You Do With It? Choosing a Vocation, Concentrated Energy, Triumph of Enthusiasm, Promptness, Appearance, Personality, Common Sense, Accuracy, Persistence, Success Under Difficulties, Observation and Self-Improvement, Triumph of the Common Virtues. 432 pgs. 5x8. Pbk. ISBN: 0-89540-331-5.

PUSHING TO THE FRONT VOL II by Orison Swett Marden. The Man With an Idea, The Will and the Way, Work and Wait, Might of Little Things, Expect Great Things of Yourself, Stand for Something, Habit: Servant or Master, Power of Purity, Power of Suggestion, Conquest of Poverty, Home as a School of Good Manners, Thrift, Why Some Succeed and Others Fail, Character is Power, Rich Without Money. 441 pgs. 5x8. Pbk. ISBN: 0-89540-332-3.

PUSHING TO THE FRONT - TWO VOL. SET by Orison Swett Marden. 873 pgs. ISBN: 0-89540-333-1.

RISING IN THE WORLD OR ARCHITECTS OF FATE by Orison Swett Marden. 318 pgs. 5x8. Pbk. ISBN: 0-89540-375-7.

THE SECRET OF ACHIEVEMENT by Orison Swett Marden. Moral Sunshine, "Blessed Be Drudgery", Honesty - As Principle and As Policy, Habit: The Servant or The Master, Courage, Self-Control, & the School of Life, Decide, Tenacity of Purpose, The Art of Keeping Well, Purity is Power, Etc. 301 pgs. 5x8. Pbk. ISBN: 0-89540-337-4.

SELLING THINGS by Orison Swett Marden. The Man Who Can Sell Things, Training the Salesman, Making a Favorable Impression, The Selling Talk or "Presentation", How to Get Attention, Friend - Winner and Business-Getter, Sizing Up the Prospect, How Suggestion Helps in Selling, The Gentle Art of Persuasion, Closing the Deal, Enthusiasm, Meeting and Forestalling Objections, Finding Customers, When You are Discouraged, Know Your Goods, Character is Capital, Keeping Fit and Salesmanship, Etc. 276 pgs. 5x8. Pbk. ISBN: 0-89540-339-0.

STORIES FROM LIFE A BOOK FOR YOUNG PEOPLE by Orison Swett Marden. 240 pgs. 5x8. Pbk. ISBN: 0-89540-411-7.

SUCCESS NUGGETS by Orison Swett Marden. Inspiration, Positive Thinking, Self-help, Business. 76 pgs. 5x8. Pbk. ISBN: 0-89540-354-4.

TALKS WITH GREAT WORKERS by Orison Swett Marden. 110 pgs. 5x8. Pbk. ISBN: 0-89540-402-8.

THRIFT by Orison Swett Marden. 92 pgs.5x8. Pbk. ISBN:0-89540-393-5.

TRAINING FOR EFFICIENCY by Orison Swett Marden. 360 pgs. 5x8. Pbk. ISBN: 0-89540-394-3.

THE VICTORIOUS ATTITUDE by Orison Swett Marden. Inspiration, Positive Thinking, Self-Help, Business. 358 pgs. 5x8. Pbk. ISBN: 0-89540-353-6.

WHY GROW OLD? by Orison Swett Marden. Marden instructs his reader to "hold to youthful, buoyant thought" and keep the imagination alive and flexible. Recognizing that we may be slaves to our attitudes, this text encourages us to make as much of ourselves as possible and in doing so watch as our lives are prolonged. 30 pgs. 5x8. Pbk. ISBN: 0-89540-340-4.

WINNING OUT, A Book for Young People on Character Building by Habit Forming by Orison Swett Marden. 251 pgs. 5x8. Pbk. ISBN: 0-89540-377-3.

YOU CAN, BUT WILL YOU? by Orison Swett Marden. The Magic Mirror, The New Philosophy of Life, Connecting With the Power that Creates, You Can, But Will You? How Do You Stand With Yourself? The New Philosophy in Business, What Are You Thinking? Facing Life the Right Way, How to Realize Your Ambition, The Open Door, Do You Carry Victory in Your Face? 338 pgs. 5x8. Pbk. ISBN: 0-89540-342-0.

THE YOUNG MAN ENTERING BUSINESS by Orison Swett Marden. 307 pgs. 5x8. Pbk. ISBN: 0-89540-378-1.

RALPH WALDO TRINE

CHARACTER BUILDING THOUGHT POWER by Ralph Waldo Trine. "Have we within our power to determine at all times what types of habits shall take form in our lives? In other words, is habit-forming, character-building, a matter of mere chance, or do we have it within our control?" 51 pgs. 5x8. Pbk. ISBN 0-89540-251-3.

EVERY LIVING CREATURE or Heart Training Through the Animal World, by Ralph Waldo Trine. The tender and humane passion in the human heart is too precious a quality to allow it to be hardened or effaced by practices such as we often indulge in. 50 pgs. 5x8. Pbk. ISBN 0-89540-309-9.

THE GREATEST THING EVER KNOWN by Ralph Waldo Trine. The Greatest Thing Ever Known, Divine Energies in Every-Day Life, The Master's Great but Lost Gift, The Philosopher's Ripest Life Thought, Sustained in Peace and Safety Forever. 57 pgs. 5x8. Pbk. ISBN 0-89540-274-2.

THE HIGHER POWERS OF MIND AND SPIRIT by Ralph Waldo Trine. The Silent, Subtle Building Forces of Mind and Spirit, Thought as a Force in Daily Living, The Divine Rule in the Mind and Heart, The Powerful Aid of the Mind In Rebuilding Body-How Body Helps Mind, Etc. 240 pgs. 5x8. Pbk. ISBN 0-89540-278-5.

IN THE FIRE OF THE HEART by Ralph Waldo Trine. With the People: A Revelation, The Conditions that Hold Among Us, As Time Deals with Nations, As to Government, A Great People's Movement, Public Utilities for the Public Good, Labour and Its Uniting Power, Agencies Whereby We Shall Secure the People's Greatest Good, The Great Nation, The Life of the Higher Beauty and Power. 338 pgs. 6x8 Pbk. ISBN 0-89540-310-2.

IN THE HOLLOW OF HIS HAND by Ralph Waldo Trine. The Present Demand to Know the Truth, The Thought - The Existing Conditions and the Religions of Jesus' Time, What Jesus Realized, Jesus' Own Statement of the Essence of Religion, Was the Church Sanctioned or Established by

Jesus?, Our Debt to the Prophets of Israel, The Power - The Beauty - and the Sustaining Peace. 242 pgs. 5x8. Pbk. ISBN 0-89540-358-7.

IN TUNE WITH THE INFINITE by Ralph Waldo Trine. A Message to My Readers, Prelude, The Supreme Fact of the Universe, The Supreme Fact of Human Life, Fullness of Life - Bodily Health and Vigor, The Secret Power and Effects of Love, Wisdom and Interior Illumination, The Realization of Perfect peace, Coming into Fullness of Power, Plenty of All Things - The Law of Prosperity, How Men Have Become Prophets, Seers, Sages, and Saviors, The Basic Principle of All Religions - The Universal Religion, Entering Now Into the Realization of the Highest Riches, Etc. 221 pgs. 5x8. Pbk. ISBN: 0-89540-387-0.

THE MAN WHO KNEW by Ralph Waldo Trine. The Power of Love, All is Well, That Superb Teaching of "Sin," He Teaches the Great Truth, When a Brave Man Chooses Death, Bigotry in Fear Condemns and Kills, Love the Law of Life, The Creative Power of Faith and Courage, Etc. 230 pgs. 5x8. Pbk. ISBN 0-89540-267-X.

MY PHILOSOPHY AND MY RELIGION by Ralph Waldo Trine. This Place: Amid the Silence of the Centuries, With the Oldest Living Things, My Philosophy, My Religion, The Creed of the Open Road. 130 pgs. 5x8. Pbk. ISBN 0.89540-349-8.

THE NEW ALIGNMENT OF LIFE by Ralph Waldo Trifle. Science and Modern Research, The Modern Spiritual Revival, The Vitalizing Power of the Master's Message, Modern Philosophic Thought, A Thinking Man's Religion, A Healthy Mind in a Healthy Body, The Mental Law of Habit. 228 pgs. 5x8. Pbk. ISBN 0-89540-347-1.

ON THE OPEN ROAD by Ralph Waldo Trine. To always clearly realize that thoughts are forces, that like creates like and like attracts like, and that to determine one's thinking therefore is to determine his life. 65 pgs. 5x8. Pbk. ISBN 0-89540-252-1.

THIS MYSTICAL LIFE OF OURS. A Book of Suggestive Thoughts for Each Week Through the Year by Ralph Waldo Trine. The Creative Power of Thought, The Laws of Attraction, Prosperity, and Habit-Forming, Faith and Prayer - Their Nature, Self-Mastery, Thoughts are Forces, How We Attract Success or Failure, The Secret and Power of Love, Will - The Human and The Divine, The Secret of the Highest Power, Wisdom or Interior Illumination, How Mind Builds Body, Intuition: The Voice of the Soul, To Be at Peace, Etc. 190 pgs. 5x8. Pbk. ISBN: 0-89540-279-3.

THROUGH THE SUNLIT YEAR by Ralph Waldo Trine. A book of Suggestive Thoughts for each day of the year from the writings of Ralph Waldo Trine. 250 pgs. 6x8. Pbk. ISBN: 0-89540-350-1.

14

WHAT ALL THE WORLD'S A-SEEKING, or the Vital Law of True Life, True Greatness, Power and Happiness by Ralph Waldo Trine. The Principle, Application, Unfoldment, Awakening, The Incoming, Character-Building Thought Power. 224 pgs. 5x8. Pbk. ISBN: 0-89540-359-5.

THE WINNING OF THE BEST by Ralph Waldo Trine. Which Way Is Life Leaning? The Creative Power of Thought, The Best Is the Life, The Power That Makes Us What We Are, A Basis of Philosophy and Religion, How We Will Win the Best. 100 pgs. 5x8. Pbk. ISBN: 0-89540-348-X.

ADDITIONAL TITLES

ACRES OF DIAMONDS by Russell H. Conwell. Through this lecture, Conwell debunks the idea that it is noble to be poor, an idea that far too many of us share. He illustrates that it is our duty as humans to use our gifts to honestly earn riches, because we can do more good with riches than without. 82 pgs. 5x8. Pbk. ISBN: 0-89540-418-4.

BEING AND BECOMING - The Principles and Practices of the Science of Spirit by Fenwicke L. Holmes. The Great Law of Mind, Concentration vs. Ideation, Affirmation, Healing Realization, The Purpose of Spirit, The Motive - Love, Love - The Healing Power, Feelings and Emotions, Why Many Fail, Mysticism, Our Power of Choice, Being, Intuition, Spirit as Formative, Demonstrating Prosperity. 50 pgs. 5x8. Pbk. ISBN: 0-89540-263-7.

THE KINGSHIP OF SELF-CONTROL by William George Jordan. The Kingship of Self-Control, The Crimes Of The Tongue, The Red Tape Of Duty, The Supreme Charity Of The World, Etc. 5x8. Pbk. ISBN: 0-89540-419-2.

THE MAJESTY OF CALMNESS by William George Jordan. The Majesty of Calmness, Hurry - the Scourge of America, The Power of Personal Influence, The Dignity of Self-Reliance, Failure as a Success, Doing Our Best at All Times, The Royal Road to Happiness. 63 pgs. 5x8. Pbk. ISBN: 0-98540-423-0.

A MESSAGE TO GARCIA and Other Essays by Elbert Hubbard. A Message to Garcia, The Boy from Missouri Valley, Help Yourself by Helping the House. "He was of big service to me in telling me the things I knew, but which I did not know I knew, until he told me." *Thomas A Edison* 48 pgs. 5x8. Pbk. ISBN: 0-89540-305-6.

POSITIVE THOUGHTS ATTRACT SUCCESS by Mary A. Dodson and Ella E. Dodson. "Unless We Can Do The Work Better, We Have No Right To Find Fault When Another Does It," "I Am a Holy Temple, and Send Out Love and Good To All The World," "What You Accomplish is Often

Determined by What You Attempt", "I will Develop a Powerful Personality," Etc. 64 pgs. 5x8. Pbk. ISBN: 0-89540-299-8.

THE SCIENCE OF GETTING RICH or Financial Success Through Thought by Wallace D. Wattles. The Right to be Rich, There is a Science to Getting Rich, How Riches Come to You, Thinking a Certain Way, How to Use the Will, Efficient Action, Getting into the Right Business, Etc. 160 pgs. 5x8. Pbk. ISBN: 0-89540-300-5.

THE SUCCESS PROCESS by Brown Landone. Five Factors Which Guarantee Success, The Process of Vivid Thinking, Tones Used in Persuading, Use of Action, Overcoming Hindrances, Developing Capacities, Securing Justice, Augmenting Your Success by Leadership, Etc. 233 pgs. 5 x 8. Hardback. ISBN: 0-89540-181-9.

VISUALIZATION AND CONCENTRATION by Fenwicke L. Holmes. The Creative Power of Mind, Metaphysics and Psychology, Mental Telepathy, Visualization and Dramatization, Concentration, How to Choose a Career. 152 pgs. 5x8. Pbk. ISBN: 0-89540-214-9.

THE HEART OF THE NEW THOUGHT by Ella Wheeler Wilcox. Let the Past Go, Thought Force, Opulence and Eternity, Morning Influences, Philosophy of Happiness, Common Sense, The Object of Life, Wisdom and Self Conquest, Concentration and Destiny, The Breath, Generosity and Balance, Etc. 92 pgs. 5x8. Pbk. ISBN: 0-89540-268-8.

YOU CAN BE WEALTHY TOO! by R.E.A. Lambert. "Wealth is nothing more nor less than common sense continuously applied to the use of small sums of money over a long period of time." Chapters include: The Secret of Wealth, The Six Foundation Stones, The Five Main Reasons for Saving, The Twelve Rules of Spending, The Seven Rules of Investment. 103 pgs. 5x8. Pbk. ISBN: 0-89540-459-1.

For current availability send e-mail to:
info@SunBooks.com
or call 505-471-5177, toll-free 877-849-0051.

✔ *Order online at SunBooks.com!*

Write to us for our Motivational Book Catalog:
Sun Publishing Co.
P.O. Box 5588-B5
Santa Fe, NM 87502-5588 USA